ICING ON THE CAKE

Food Idioms
(A Multicultural Book)

By Troon Harrison

Illustrated by Joyeeta Neogi

Language Lizard
Basking Ridge

For English audio and resources for teaching idioms, see the last page of this book.

Icing on the Cake
Copyright © 2020 Language Lizard
Published by Language Lizard
Basking Ridge, NJ 07920
info@LanguageLizard.com

Visit us at www.LanguageLizard.com

First edition 2020

Library of Congress Control Number: 2020905419

ISBN: 978-1-951787-04-2 (Print)
ISBN: 978-1-951787-05-9 (Ebook)

WHAT IS AN IDIOM?

An idiom is a phrase that says one thing but means something different. An idiom can be a quick way of saying something complicated. Knowing idioms will help you to understand and speak English fluently. This book contains idioms about food.

SELLING LIKE HOT CAKES

Meaning: Something is selling very fast

The fresh, ripe melons were so delicious they were selling like hot cakes.

A COUCH POTATO

Meaning: A person spends hours watching TV or relaxing

She worked hard all week, but on weekends she was a couch potato.

BIGGER FISH TO FRY

Meaning: Doing something that is more important

I wanted my brother to come sailing with me, but he had bigger fish to fry.

USE YOUR NOODLE

Meaning: Use your brain to figure out something for yourself

I wanted help tying my shoes, but Dad told me to use my noodle.

WAKE UP AND SMELL THE COFFEE

Meaning: Pay attention to what is actually happening

The cowboy thought it was a safe place to camp, but he needed to **wake up and smell the coffee**.

SPILL THE BEANS

Meaning: To confess and reveal a secret

When the stray puppy howled, the children had to spill the beans.

14

CRY OVER SPILLED MILK

Meaning: To be upset about something that cannot be changed

I was upset about my bike, but Mom told me not to cry over spilled milk.

APPLE OF MY EYE

Meaning: Something a person loves very much

After my camel won the race, he was the apple of my eye.

GOING BANANAS

Meaning: Acting crazy

The boy I was watching was going bananas.

TWO PEAS IN A POD

Meaning: Two people who are very similar

My children always play together, like two peas in a pod.

A GRAIN OF SALT

Meaning: To be skeptical

My hairdresser said my new hairstyle suited me, but I took her words with **a grain of salt**.

PIE IN THE SKY

Meaning: A goal that is too ambitious and may never happen

My dream of being the first person living on Mars might be **pie in the sky**.

THE BIG CHEESE

Meaning: A person who is important and powerful

The farmer owned so many goats, she thought she was **the big cheese**.

ICING ON THE CAKE

Meaning: Something which is an extra special treat

My grandfather's surprise visit was the icing on the cake.

Visit <u>www.LanguageLizard.com/Food-Idioms</u> for additional resources for teaching and learning English idioms, including:

- English audio of this book
- Multicultural lesson plans for use in the classroom or at home
- Information on the origin of the idioms in this book
- Additional food idioms with their meaning, usage, and origin
- Information on idiom translations and idioms in other languages

This book is part of the **Language Lizard Idiom Series**.

Visit **www.LanguageLizard.com** for a complete listing of the titles in this series and available languages.

www.ingramcontent.com/pod-product-compliance
Lightning Source LLC
Chambersburg PA
CBHW060902090426
42738CB00025B/3493